FRANKLIN PARK PUBLIC LIBRARY

3 1316 00453 2800

W9-AKW-368

WITHDRAWN

FRANKLIN PARK PUBLIC LIBRARY
FRANKLIN PARK, IL.

Each borrower is held responsible for all library
material drawn on his card and for fines accruing on
the same. No material will be issued until such fine
has been paid.

All injuries to library material beyond reasonable
wear and all losses shall be made good to the
satisfaction of the Librarian.

Replacement costs will be
billed after 42 days overdue.

For Pandora, who is always at my side, especially when there are dumplings
—C. C.

For my family, with whom I have shared many delicious meals
—K. W.

J-B
CHEN
453-2860

SIMON & SCHUSTER BOOKS FOR YOUNG READERS
An imprint of Simon & Schuster Children's Publishing Division
1230 Avenue of the Americas, New York, New York 10020
Text copyright © 2017 by Carrie Clickard
Illustrations copyright © 2017 by Katy Wu
All rights reserved, including the right of reproduction in whole or in part in any form.
Simon & Schuster Books for Young Readers is a trademark of Simon & Schuster, Inc.
For information about special discounts for bulk purchases, please contact Simon & Schuster Special Sales at 1-866-506-1949 or business@simonandschuster.com.
The Simon & Schuster Speakers Bureau can bring authors to your live event. For more information or to book an event, contact the Simon & Schuster Speakers Bureau at 1-866-248-3049 or visit our website at www.simonspeakers.com.
Book design by Krista Vossen
The text for this book was set in Archer.
The illustrations for this book were rendered digitally.
Manufactured in China
0617 SCP
First Edition
2 4 6 8 10 9 7 5 3 1
Library of Congress Cataloging-in-Publication Data
Names: Clickard, Carrie (Carrie L.), author. | Wu, Katy, illustrator.
Title: Dumpling dreams : how Joyce Chen brought the dumpling from Beijing to Cambridge / Carrie Clickard ; Illustrated by Katy Wu.
Description: New York : Simon & Schuster Books for Young Readers, [2017] | "A Paula Wiseman Book." | Audience: Ages 4–8. | Audience: K to grade 3. | In rhyming text.
Identifiers: LCCN 2016050754 | ISBN 9781481467070 (hardcover) | ISBN 9781481467087 (eBook)
Subjects: LCSH: Chen, Joyce—Juvenile literature. | Cooks—China—Biography—Juvenile literature. | Cooks—United States—Biography—Juvenile literature. | Cooking, Chinese—Influence—Juvenile literature.
Classification: LCC TX649.C46 C55 2017 | DDC 641.5092 [B]—dc23
LC record available at https://lccn.loc.gov/2016050754

Dumpling Dreams

How Joyce Chen Brought the Dumpling from Beijing to Cambridge

•

Written by Carrie Clickard

Illustrated by Katy Wu

WITHDRAWN

FRANKLIN PARK LIBRARY

FRANKLIN PARK, IL

A Paula Wiseman Book

Simon & Schuster Books for Young Readers

New York London Toronto Sydney New Delhi

A quiet room.
One ink-stained girl
determined to perfect each curl.

Her writing brush
sweeps down the rows.
A scrumptious scent slips
past her nose.

Dumplings!

Jia's favorite treat.
Cook hands her one, still warm, to eat.

"You're old enough.
Come learn from me."

She climbs a stool so she can see.

Yi,
uhr,
san.

Cook rolls the dough.
Dab of stuffing. Pinch it closed.

One,

two,

three.

To Jia's shame,
her dumpling isn't
quite the same.

She practices
from spring to fall.

Dumplings,

noodles,

sweet rice balls.

Next New Year
Jia's greatest prize
is in Cook's proud,
approving eyes.

Light the lanterns.

Dragon dances.

Try a riddle.

Take your chances.

Jia's grown enough
to play,
but cooking's better
any day.

Dragon boats
race down the lake.
Jia has *zongzi* to make.

Tie them tight
with five bright strings.
Praise from Father—her heart sings!

She loves to learn,
a joy each day!

"Let's call her Joyce,"
the teachers say.

Joyce

She likes the name.
"Jia" is gone
and she is Joyce from that day on.

A red silk dress.
Tangyuan to eat.
Embroidered slippers
on her feet.

Joyce becomes
a loving wife:
new husband, city,
and new life!

Red eggs
celebrate a boy.
Dreams of moon cakes,
luck, and joy.

Then a daughter
joins the three.
A plump, delicious family.

Troubles come.
War in the news.
The heart of China split in two.

Days of worry,
nights of fear—
even dumplings taste of tears.

Is it safe?
How long before
her family's hurt by
China's war?

Joyce packs up
and sails away
from all her dumpling
dreams and days.

Two weeks
and half a world spin by.

New words to learn.

Strange food to try.

When she's scared,
heart thumps, throat tight.
The smell of dumplings
sets things right.

Cambridge bursts
with students learning.
Far from China,
filled with yearning.

Joyce invites them:
"Come and eat!"
Sharing news and
homemade treats.

Two small chairs
will soon be three.
A new son joins the family.

Stretching noodles
straight and thin
to wish long life and luck for them.

School bake sale!
A nervous day.

Joyce stacks cookies on a tray.
Egg rolls too—
a crispy tower.
Sauce for dipping, sweet and sour.

Rows of muffins,
pies, and cake.
Were her egg rolls a mistake?

Time to leave!
Face pink with shame.
People call out Joyce's name.

"Delicious egg rolls!"

"I ate four!"

"We sold out. Can you make more?"

Cheeks and bellies
stuffed with bliss.

"In Cambridge no one cooks
like this!"

Friends and family all agree
a restaurant is what Joyce needs!

A perfect spot on Concord Street where Cambridge friends can stop and eat.

JOYCE CHEN
RESTAURANT

CHINESE FOOD

TAKE OUT

It only needs one small touch more—
her name in red above the door.

Grand opening!
Joyce feels so proud.
Tables full—a hungry crowd.

No one tries
her favorite treat.
Chop suey's all they want to eat.

~~Chinese Gnocchi~~

~~Shanghai Pockets~~

Peking Ravioli

"My dumplings
aren't a gluey stew.
I need to call them something NEW!"

The name she picks
makes people smile:

Ravioli—Peking style!

Dumplings dance right out the door!

Chefs?
She needs a dozen more!
But cook like Joyce?
No one knows how.

Joyce must be the teacher now.

Measure, test,
and taste each bite,
till the recipe is right.

Write them down.
The pile grows.

A cookbook and . . .

... a TV show!

"*Ni hao!*
Come and cook with me,
my favorite dumpling recipe!"

Success has come for all to see:

an author, chef, and
mom of three!

Days filled with what
Joyce loves to do.
Her dumpling dreams have
all come true.

September 14, 1917—Liao Jia-ai (Joyce) is born in Beijing, the youngest of nine children.

1927—Civil war begins in China between people loyal to the government of China, called the Kuomintang, and those who support the Communist Party of China led by Mao Zedong.

1930s—Joyce's family moves to Shanghai.

1937—China goes to war with Japan. The conflicts within China are set aside temporarily.

1943—Joyce marries Thomas Chen in Hangzhou, China.

1944—Joyce's first son, Henry, is born.

1945—The war with Japan ends, only for the civil war to begin again.

1948—Joyce's daughter, Helen, is born.

November 23, 1948–January 6, 1949—The Huaihai campaign, a long and bloody battle in northern China, takes place. Over 1.5 million Chinese lose their lives. The Communist Party troops prepare to cross the Yangtze River. People in southern China who can afford tickets board trains and boats, hoping to escape before the army reaches their cities.

April 6, 1949—Joyce and her family set sail from Shanghai for San Francisco.

April 21, 1949—Joyce and her family settle in Cambridge, Massachusetts.

May 12–June 2, 1949—The fighting reaches Shanghai, the largest city in China. Eight thousand lives are lost as the Communist party wins control of the city.

October 1949—The Communist party captures Beijing and declares victory. The war in China ends. Mao announces the new People's Republic of China.

1952—Joyce's youngest child, Stephen, is born.

LIFE AND SUCCESS

1957—Joyce's egg rolls are a hit at Buckingham School's bake sale.

1958—The Joyce Chen Restaurant opens for business.

1958—Peking Ravioli debuts as item #4 on the menu.

1960—Joyce begins teaching Chinese cooking classes at the Boston Center for Adult Education.

1962—Her cookbook, *Joyce Chen Cook Book*, is published.

1966—Joyce divorces Thomas Chen.

1967—A second restaurant, The J C Small Eating Place, opens.

1967—Her TV show on PBS, *Joyce Chen Cooks*, debuts in the US, UK, and Australia.

1968—Joyce takes Stephen and Helen back to China where *Joyce Chen's China* is filmed.

1970—Her third restaurant, seating 500 people, opens.

1971—Joyce launches her own line of cooking utensils—woks, steamers, knives, and more!

1973—*Time Magazine* profiles Joyce Chen, calling her "Fortune's Cookie."

1976—Joyce cuts her hand badly, requiring surgery, from which she never fully recovers.

1982—J C Specialty Foods opens—now everyone can enjoy Joyce's food at home, too!

1984—Joyce attends a White House dinner with President Reagan and the Chinese Premiere.

1985—Joyce is diagnosed with Alzheimer's disease.

August 23, 1994—Joyce passes away after a nine-year battle with Alzheimer's disease.

1998—Joyce is inducted into the James Beard Hall of Fame.

2014—Joyce is immortalized on a US postage stamp.

GLOSSARY

Chop suey: Chopped vegetables stir-fried with sliced meat, served over rice. Chop suey is thought to have been first cooked in Chinese communities in California in the 1840s.

Dragon dance: A folk dance performed by a team of dancers who carry a long, flexible paper or silk dragon on tall poles. Dragon dances are performed to celebrate many Chinese festivals, including New Year.

Dumplings (Peking Ravioli): Small pockets of dough filled with pork or vegetables, folded into half-moon shapes, and then deep-fried or steamed. Joyce Chen gave them their famous nickname, Peking Ravioli, because ravioli is also a small pocket of dough stuffed with meat or cheese and Peking (Beijing) is the capital of China. These dumplings are known as *guo tie* in China.

Egg rolls: Crispy deep-fried wrappers stuffed with chicken, pork, or shrimp with cabbage, bean sprouts, and other vegetables.

Embroidered slippers: A wedding tradition in China. In Mandarin the word for shoes is "xie" which sounds like the word for harmony. Shoes also come in pairs, like a bride and groom. A bride's slippers are often embroidered with the symbols for "double joy" and peony flowers for luck.

Moon cakes: Round flaky cakes filled with sweet lotus paste and a salted duck egg. When the cake is cut, the yoke of the egg looks like the moon. Each region of China has its own unique version of moon cake. Moon cakes are eaten during the Mid-Autumn Festival, when Joyce's first son Henry was born.

Ni hao: "Hello" in Mandarin

Noodles: On birthdays in China people often eat noodles stretched out long and thin. The longer the noodle, the longer the birthday boy or girl will live.

Peking: When Joyce Chen moved to Cambridge, people in the United States spelled the capital city of China "Peking," so she called her dumplings "Peking Ravioli." Today, we use "Beijing," which is the accepted spelling of the Mandarin word. The name of the city didn't change, just the way we translate it from Chinese hanzi characters into our English alphabet.

Red eggs: In China the color red symbolizes happiness. Eggs represent a new beginning or a fresh start. A new baby is a very happy beginning, so births are often celebrated with a *moon-yut,* a red egg party.

Sweet rice balls: Round pastry made of rice, sugar, and coconut powder and stuffed with sweet filling.

Tangyuan: Plump rice balls stuffed with red bean, black sesame, or other sweet fillings.

Yi, uhr, san: Counting "one, two, three" in Mandarin.

Zongzi: Sticky rice wrapped in bamboo leaves and tied with string into a triangle shape. *Zhong zhi* are served at the Dragon Boat Festival which is held on the fifth day of the fifth month.

BIBLIOGRAPHY

These books, videos, and articles will help you learn more about Joyce Chen, her family, and her wonderful Peking Ravioli.

COOKBOOKS BY JOYCE AND HER DAUGHTER HELEN

Chen, Joyce (1962). *Joyce Chen Cook Book*. Philadelphia & New York: J. B. Lippincott, 1962.

Chen, Helen (1994). *Helen Chen's Chinese Home Cooking*. New York: William Morrow.

VIDEOS

Joyce Chen Cooks. Several episodes of her cooking show are available to view online at WGBH's web archive openvault.wgbh.org

Joyce Chen's China. Travel documentary, WGBH Boston, 1973. This video is available to researchers.

ARTICLES & INTERVIEWS ABOUT JOYCE

"Fortune's Cookie," *Time Magazine*, January 29, 1973.

"Joyce Chen, 76, U.S. Popularizer of Mandarin Cuisine." *New York Times*. August 26, 1994.

"Joyce Chen (1917-1994)—National Women's History Museum." http://www.nwhm.org/education-resources/biography/biographies/joyce-chen/

Robertson, Rain. "Joyce Chen." *Culinary Cambridge*. Cambridge Historical Society http://cambridgehistory.org/discover/culinary/joycechen.html

Daley, Bill. "Taught American palates to speak Chinese." *Chicago Tribune*. February 20, 2013.

Seltzer, Anne-Marie. "Helen Chen Remembers her Mother." http://patch.com/massachusetts/lexington/helen-chen-remembers-her-mother

"Five Celebrity Chefs Immortalized on Limited Edition Forever Stamps." United States Postal Service. http://about.usps.com/news/national-releases/2014/pr14_050.htm

Dreaming of cooking up your own dumplings? Find a grown-up and have them help you make this fun and tasty recipe.

Ingredients

For dumplings:
1 package pre-made wonton wrappers

Very Veggie Filling: Pick and mix your favorite three
Rainbow shredded coleslaw (shredded cabbage can be substituted)
Julienne-cut carrots
Chopped spinach
Corn (canned)
Finely chopped broccoli
Mushrooms, diced

Moist and Meaty Filling: Mix ahead & refrigerate
½ lb ground pork, chicken or turkey
2 scallions or green onions, finely sliced
1½ tsp soy sauce
¼ tsp pepper
½ tsp sesame oil (optional)
1 egg, beaten

For dipping sauce:
2 Tbsp soy sauce
1 tsp sugar
1 Tbsp rice wine vinegar
2 drops sesame oil
(Minced garlic or ginger can be added for a stronger flavor)